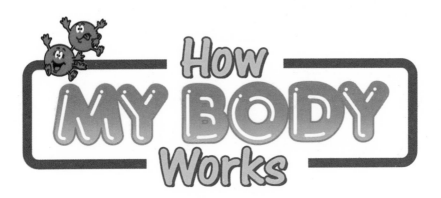

How
MY BODY
Works

The
Skin

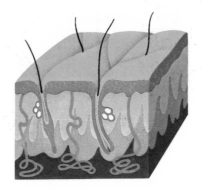

Your Skin

What's your skin for?

The skin is the largest of the body's organs. On average, an adult has about 2sq.m of skin. Your skin fits you whatever size you grow to. The skin keeps your whole body together and does many other jobs as well.

● It helps to control the temperature of your body – it keeps you warm or cool.

● It is waterproof; it keeps you dry.

● The skin protects you from harmful things like poisons, diseases and the sun's ultra-violet rays. Diseases can only get through the skin where it is broken.

● The skin is where you feel things such as cold, heat or pain. The skin contains the nerve endings that give you your sense of touch so that when you feel an object you can tell what it is made of and what size it is.

● The skin builds up Vitamin D, which helps your bones to grow strongly.

● The skin stores fat.

● It can absorb oxygen and release carbon dioxide.

Infections

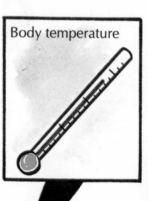

Body temperature

Sense of touch

Waterproof

The Professor directs the body's defence system. He and Metro, his lieutenant, work to protect your body. Globus and his team of red blood cells need protection as they travel the body delivering oxygen. So Captain Courageous, chief of the white corpuscles and his friends Ace and Corpo cruise around the body attacking their enemies Virulus, the virus and Toxicus, the bacterium.

CONTENTS

What's your skin like?

Your skin is both firm and flexible and it can expand and contract. It is designed so that you can move easily. Your skin is loose and wrinkly on your elbows so that you can bend them. It is tight and firm on your feet so that you can walk without sliding around.

Most of your skin is about 1.5mm thick. But this varies, for example, the eyelids are only about 0.5mm thick, but the skin on the soles of our feet – which take a lot of battering – may be up to 6mm thick.

The skin breathes through many tiny openings called pores. Hairs grow through the skin all over your body, except on the soles of your feet and the palms of your hands. Your skin can be divided into three closely packed layers: the epidermis, the dermis and a fatty layer known as the hypodermis.

The palms of your hands, your fingers and the soles of your feet are covered in minute ridges and grooves which make patterns. The patterns on your fingertips are unique to you – no-one else has the same patterns. If fingerprints are found at the scene of a crime, they help the police to identify the criminal because no-one else has the same prints.

The epidermis – the surface of your skin

The top layer of your skin, the one that you see, is called the epidermis. It is dry and waterproof and protects your body from infections and prevents it drying out and shrivelling up. The very top layer of the epidermis is made of flat, dead cells. These dead cells are constantly rubbed off. Did you know that most house dust is flakes of dead skin that have rubbed off people's bodies? The epidermis is constantly producing new cells to make new skin. It also contains the coloured substance which gives the skin its colour.

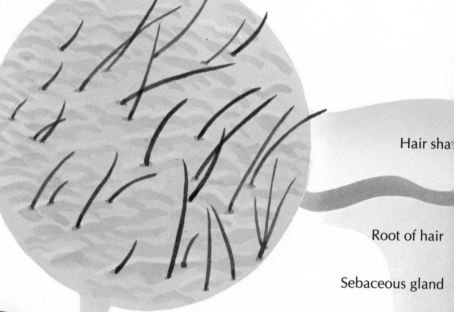

Hair sha

Root of hair

Sebaceous gland

If you examine the skin on the back of your hand through a magnifying glass, you'll discover a scene like a rugged landscape, spiked with prickles and spines. The surface grooves wind their way around 'craters' – the sweat pores. The spikes that look like dark spines or grass blades are, in fact, hairs. The younger you are, the finer and thinner the hairs. That's why you can hardly see them without a magnifying glass.

The dermis and the hypodermis

The layer below the epidermis is called the dermis. The dermis gives your skin its stretchiness. It is made of elastic fibres, which help your skin to expand and contract. The dermis contains many blood vessels, which keep the skin supplied with food and oxygen. There are numerous nerve endings (sensory receptors) in the dermis. They send messages to the central nervous system because they are sensitive to pain, pressure, cold and warmth. Under the dermis lies the third layer – the hypodermis. It contains fat, which helps to keep you warm, and helps to protect you. The hypodermis also stores energy and connects your skin with your bones and your muscles.

As well as nerve endings, elastic fibres and blood vessels the dermis contains hair follicles that produce hairs. Each hair has a tiny muscle that makes it stand on end or lie flat. The sebaceous glands produce oil that keeps your skin supple and conditions your hair. The sweat glands in the dermis make salty sweat to help cool the surface of the skin.

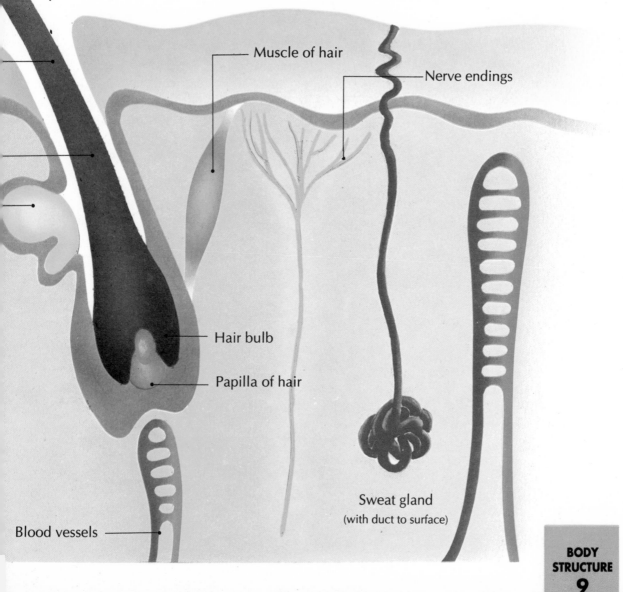

Muscle of hair

Nerve endings

Hair bulb

Papilla of hair

Sweat gland
(with duct to surface)

Blood vessels

What does the sun do to your skin?

Your skin contains a substance called melanin, which protects your skin and gives it its colour. If you have a lot of melanin, your skin will be very dark brown or black; if you have very little, your skin will be fair. Your skin protects your body from the sun's harmful rays by producing more melanin, which tans your skin. The more melanin you produce, the deeper your suntan. But it is not a good idea to expose your skin to a lot of sun. Scientists have discovered that it can cause skin cancer. But the sun can be helpful: in the sun your skin makes Vitamin D which helps your bones to grow healthily.

Hairs – growing from your skin

Hairs grow on every part of your body except the palms of your hands and the soles of your feet. An adult usually has about 100,000 head hairs and each one grows about 12cm a year. Hairs can last quite a long time; a hair on your head may grow for up to four years before it falls out. But an eyelash lasts only about six months.

If you pull out one of your hairs, you feel a sharp pain, but cutting your hair doesn't hurt at all. Why is that? The answer is simple: a hair is only alive at the root. This area is very sensitive. If it is pulled or torn, the nerves react by sending messages of pain to your brain. But the hair itself is dead. Each hair shaft consists of overlapping horny scales made of keratin, which is a substance rather like your nails. So when your hair is cut you don't feel any pain.

A hair grows inside a tube called a follicle, which can be in the dermis or hypodermis. At the bottom of each follicle are cells which are fed by blood vessels. The cells make the hair from keratin, a kind of protein.

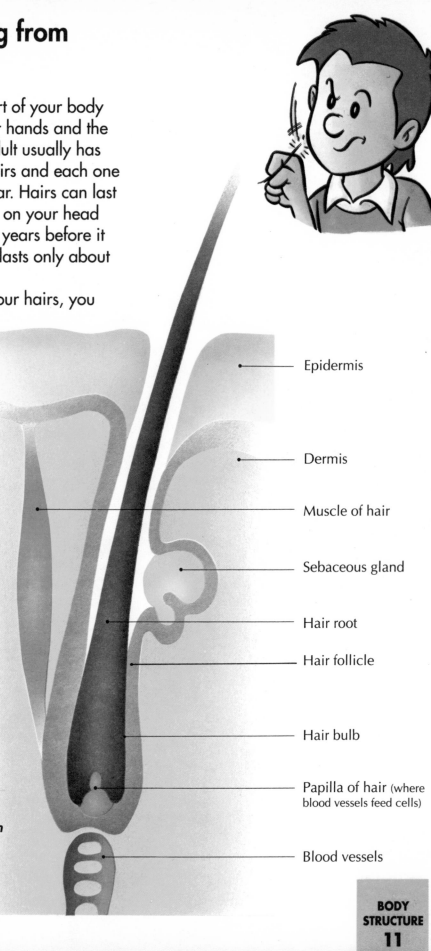

Epidermis

Dermis

Muscle of hair

Sebaceous gland

Hair root

Hair follicle

Hair bulb

Papilla of hair (where blood vessels feed cells)

Blood vessels

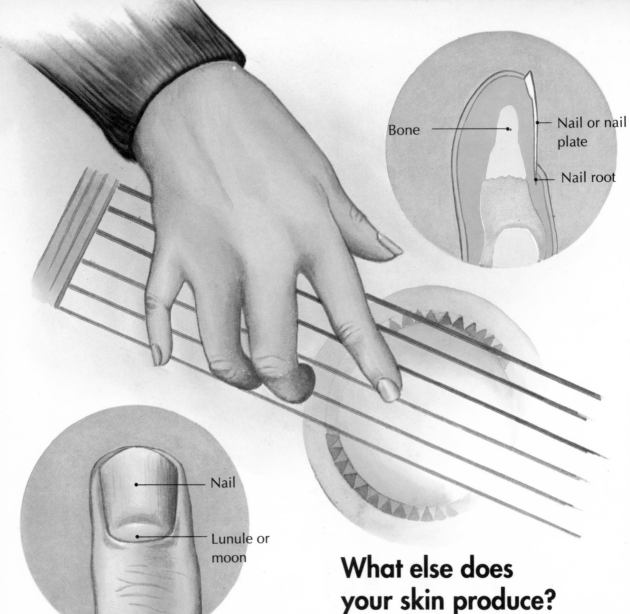

Bone

Nail or nail plate

Nail root

Nail

Lunule or moon

Nails are hard – very important for guitarists! The tips of the nails are much harder than the roots, which are really quite soft and are embedded under the skin. The root is alive; it is where the nail grows from. A completely new nail takes several months to grow. You can cut the hard, insensitive nail tips without feeling any pain.

What else does your skin produce?

The delicate tips of your fingers and toes are protected by nails. Like hairs, nails are dead cells with keratin in them to make them hard. Your nails grow all the time. If you did not cut them, they would grow about 4cm in a year.

The skin also produces an oily substance in the sebaceous glands. This keeps hair and skin moist and elastic, without it your skin would feel tight, dry and itchy. Sometimes, especially when you are a teenager, the sebaceous glands produce too much oil and your hair and skin can get very greasy.

NO SWEAT!

When you get hot, you sweat. Sweat is a mixture of water, salt and other substances made in the sweat glands and it helps to cool your body down. When you are hot it comes out through the pores on to your skin. As it evaporates, it cools your skin. Your skin has 3,000,000 sweat glands. If you lined them all up, they would stretch for 48km. On a warm day, these glands produce about 300ml of sweat. On a very hot day, an adult's sweat glands may produce up to 2.5 litres. The skin has another way of keeping cool. When you get hot, the blood comes to the surface of the skin where the air can cool it down. That's why your skin sometimes looks red when you are hot.

The hotter, the sweatier... With rising temperature the sweat glands become more active, pumping more and more sweat to the open pores on the skin's surface. Sweat consists mainly of water (99%) and of mineral salts (less than 1%). These minerals make your skin taste salty when you're sweating. Your sweat glands keep your body from overheating. You can sweat when you exercise, or when you are very frightened. Besides helping to cool your body, sweat coats the skin with an acidic layer which helps to protect it from bacteria.

How Your Skin Senses Things

'Seeing' by touching

If you have ever played the party game where you put on a blindfold and feel things with your fingers, you will know that you can tell what things are simply by touching them. When your fingers touch an object, the nerve endings (sensory receptors) in the skin receive messages about it (sensations). The messages record what it feels like: what sort of shape it is, whether it is hard or soft, rough or smooth, hot or cold. The messages are sent to the brain through the nerves. When they arrive a split second later, the brain interprets them and decides what you are

touching. The message in the picture below would be: 'This is a box.'

Your skin is your biggest sense organ and you have millions of nerve endings, or receptors, all over your body, near the surface of your skin. Through them you can feel the slightest touch of a feather as well as a heavy brick dropped on your big toe.

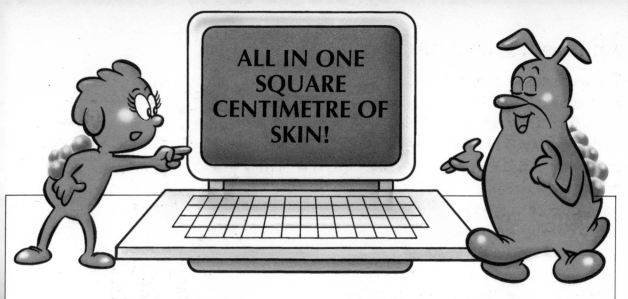

ALL IN ONE SQUARE CENTIMETRE OF SKIN!

If you could follow Captain Courageous and Ace on a journey through one square centimetre of skin, you would be astonished at all the incredible things you would see.

In that tiny space you would find a network of amazing mechanisms, including those that control temperature, that sense things by touch and those that feed the skin.

● 1 metre of blood vessels, which form a network taking blood to every part of the skin

● up to 200 hairs, which are constantly growing – but not on the palms of your hands or the soles of your feet

● 15 sebaceous glands, which keep your skin and hair oiled and supple

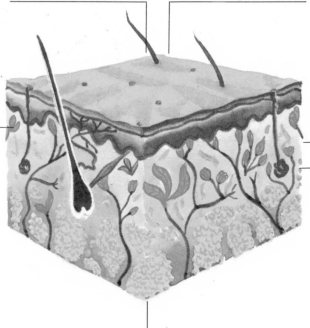

● about 230 nerve endings, which record the sensations of pain, pressure and temperature and send messages to the brain

● 100 sweat glands regulating your body temperature

● 4 metres of nerves, which take messages to the brain

All about nerve endings

There are many different nerve endings in your skin and they are all vitally important. They can sense pain, heat, cold and pressure. Together they send a pattern of coded messages to your brain which deciphers them and decides how to react to the sensations that the nerve endings are reporting.

   If you get rather hot because you have been out in the sun or running around playing a game, the nerve endings in your skin will send messages to your brain and it will take the appropriate action. It may expand the blood vessels near the surface of the skin so that more blood is close to the surface and can be cooled by the air. Your brain may also activate the sweat glands to send sweat pouring to the surface of the skin to evaporate and so cool it down.

The different types of nerve endings (sensory receptors) are very different in shape. Scientists used to think that each kind was responsible for sensing either heat or cold, pressure or pain, but today it is thought that they can all react together. Each one is named after the scientist who discovered them:

Nerve endings

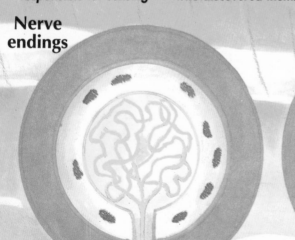

Krause end bulb

Pacinian corpuscle

Ruffini corpuscle

Hot or cold?

With our temperature sensitive receptors we can detect the difference between hot and cold. For instance, if you put your left hand in warm water and your right hand in cold water at the same time, you'll feel a distinct difference. If you then put both hands into tepid water immediately after, your left hand will feel a cold sensation, and your right hand a warm sensation. So we don't feel the exact temperature, we just react to the difference.

If you get cold, the nerve endings will feel it before you do! They will send messages to your brain saying 'cold'. When the message reaches the brain you will feel cold. A different part of your brain may then tell the little muscles attached to each hair on your body to contract and pull the hair upright. This traps warm air between the hairs and helps your skin to keep warm. That's why you get goose pimples when you are cold.

At the tips of your fingers

You understand the world around you not only through your eyes and ears, but also through your sense of touch. Nerve endings enable you to feel objects. Some areas of your body, such as the tips of your fingers and toes and the tip of your tongue, are more sensitive than others. That's because the nerve endings are very close together in these areas, especially one called Meissner's corpuscle. There are about 100-200 of them per square centimetre. Thanks to these tiny sensory receptors, you can even feel the beat of a butterfly's wing on your skin.

Captain Courageous and Ace are on patrol through the dermis. They're making sure that the Meissner's corpuscles are working properly: are they transmitting all the messages from the skin to the brain?

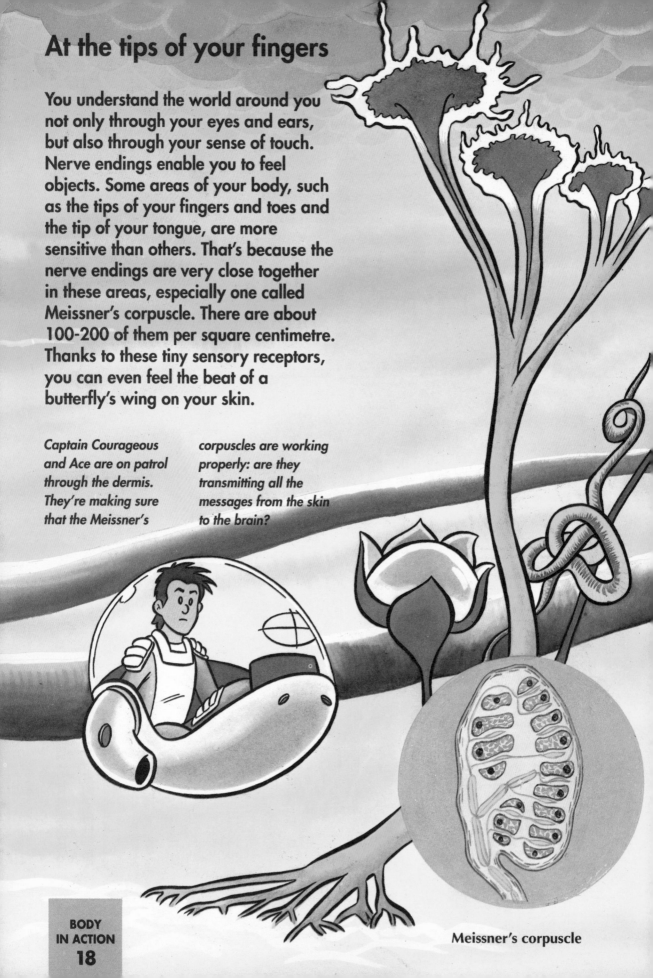

Meissner's corpuscle

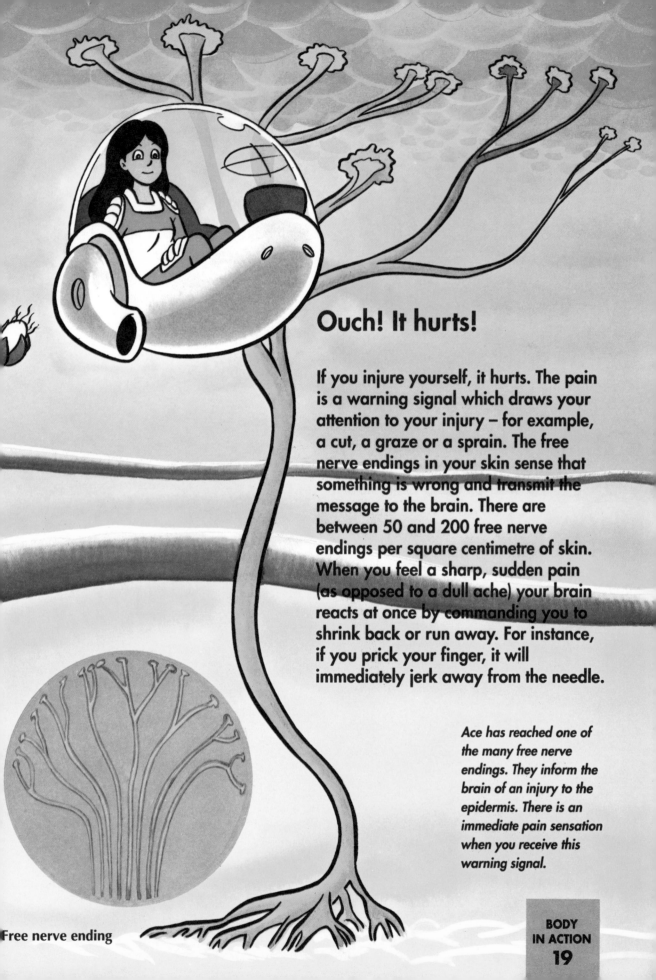

Ouch! It hurts!

If you injure yourself, it hurts. The pain is a warning signal which draws your attention to your injury – for example, a cut, a graze or a sprain. The free nerve endings in your skin sense that something is wrong and transmit the message to the brain. There are between 50 and 200 free nerve endings per square centimetre of skin. When you feel a sharp, sudden pain (as opposed to a dull ache) your brain reacts at once by commanding you to shrink back or run away. For instance, if you prick your finger, it will immediately jerk away from the needle.

Ace has reached one of the many free nerve endings. They inform the brain of an injury to the epidermis. There is an immediate pain sensation when you receive this warning signal.

Free nerve ending

Your Skin's Defences

Getting through the armour

The skin is like a suit of armour which protects you against harmful bacteria. But if there is even the slightest chink in the armour, such as a graze or cut, harmful micro-organisms (germs) can get through and infect your body. How exactly does infection begin? If you got a nail stuck in your hand, the wound might get infected. This is because the nail would probably be covered with dirt which contains many germs. Once the nail has broken the skin, the microscopic germs can get under the surface and cause an infection. If they succeed, the wound will hurt and become hot, red, and swollen – the major signs of an infection.

Your body's defence system will immediately go into action to fight the infection. The harmful germs are attacked by one of the body's defence mechanisms: the phagocytes. The phagocytes literally 'eat up' the invaders and kill them. Once the body's defence mechanisms have won the battle and destroyed all the harmful invaders, the wound can begin to heal.

If germs manage to get through the skin a whole army of phagocytes is waiting for them in the blood vessels. The phagocytes rush to the rescue and start to *swallow the invaders. One of the defending army is Corpo, the white cell. Corpo and his friends are champion eaters and can destroy armies of harmful germs.*

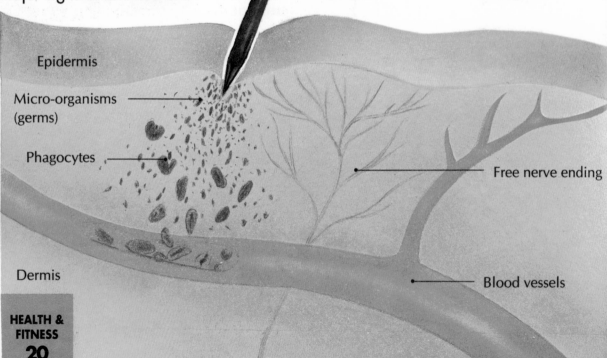

Epidermis

Micro-organisms (germs)

Phagocytes

Free nerve ending

Dermis

Blood vessels

Corpo in action - he shows how phagocytes gobble up germs. In the picture below you can see the macrophages attacking germs under a microscope. They look enormous as they swallow the invading germs.

Fighting infection

When the germs manage to get through the skin they give off their own special poisons called toxins. Phagocytes like toxins, so they seize the invaders, gobble them up, digest them and neutralize them. The body's defence system has two lines of defence. The first into battle are the small white blood cells which are found in the bloodstream. They rush to the injured spot and do what they can. If a few of the invaders escape them, bigger cells called the macrophages are brought up from the rear, like tanks in battle. Your body's natural defences can deal with minor illnesses and injuries, but in case of serious infections it needs outside help. That's when the doctor may prescribe medicines called antibiotics to fight the infection.

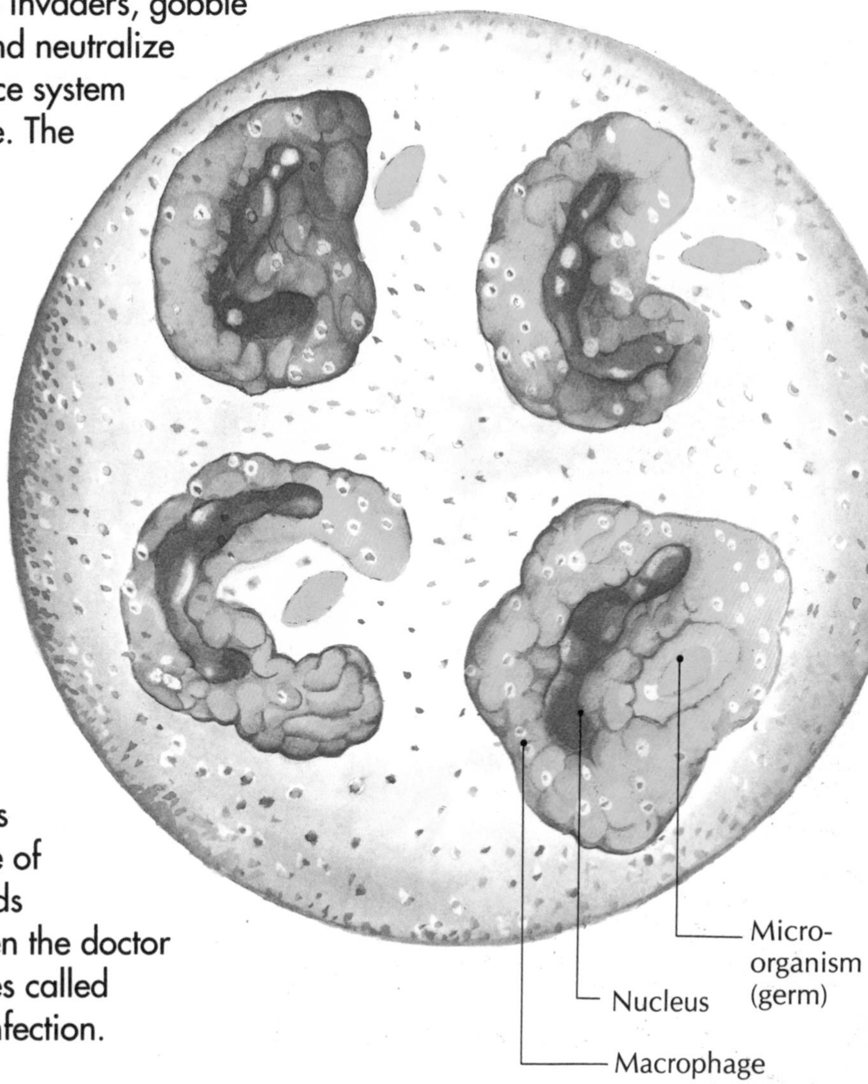

Micro-organism (germ)

Nucleus

Macrophage

Insect attack

Some insects just love the taste of blood. They live by sucking blood from other animals including humans. You've probably been bitten by a mosquito and know how itchy the bite can be. So what happens when an insect, such as a mosquito, bites you? A mosquito's mouth is like a long tube. When the insect lands on you, it pierces your skin with the tube and sucks your blood up through the tube. At the same time it leaves saliva (spit) in your skin. Your body doesn't like this much and reacts against it. The area around the bite swells up and it begins to itch. Eventually the body's defence system fights the germs that the insect has left in your skin and the bite heals.

Stings are different from bites. Insects, such as bees and wasps, defend themselves from larger animals by injecting venom (poison) into the skin. The venom causes swelling, redness and pain for up to 48 hours, but you can use special creams to ease the symptoms.

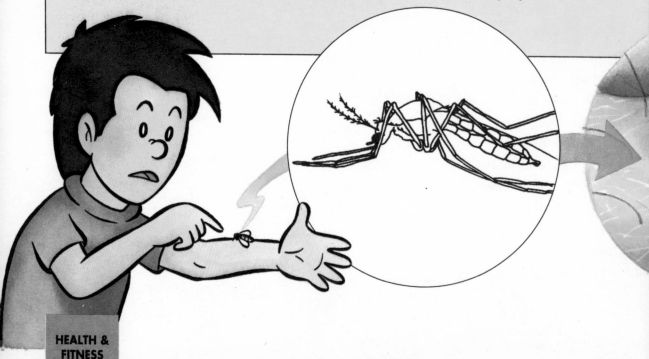

How your skin heals itself

If you cut, or injure yourself in any way, germs may get into your body and cause an infection. Sometimes an infected cut or graze gets pus in it. Pus is a thick, yellowish liquid made by your body and it contains white blood cells. So pus is actually part of the healing process; it helps in fighting the infection.

However large or small a wound is, your body will set about mending the hole in your skin. First, the repair cells in your blood create a net across the wound. Blood cells bunch up behind the net and form a blood clot. The clotted blood dries and forms a scab which seals the skin. The scab prevents blood getting out and more germs getting in. Meanwhile, the body starts to grow new skin under the scab. It begins to grow from the edges of the wound. When it has grown right across, the scab drops off and the skin is whole again.

When you are bitten by an insect it can be so itchy that the temptation to scratch is enormous. But try not to, otherwise you may end up like Toxicus. If you scratch the bite you may get dirt in it and it may become infected and get bigger and last much longer. Your body's defence system will do the work much better. The phagocytes will eat the germs up and the bite will heal by itself. It's much better to bear the itch and apply a soothing ointment.

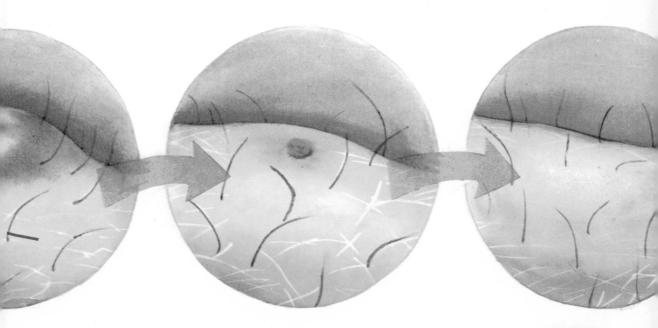

Take care of your skin!

Your skin is covered in a very thin coating of sebum. Sebum is oily; it keeps your skin moist and supple and prevents it drying out. Sebum also contains acid, which helps to protect the skin from germs. Sebum is made in the skin's sebaceous glands. Most of the time they produce exactly the right amount of sebum for your skin, but when you are a teenager they sometimes produce too much and your skin becomes very oily. This can cause acne, because the hair follicles get blocked with sebum and

Your skin can get very dirty in a day. Dirt sticks to the thin coating of oil and stale sweat can cover the surface. Washing regularly with soap and water helps to clean germs from the skin and prevent infection – as well as nasty smells! Use gentle soap if your skin is dry.

become infected. Acne spots are not easy to cure, but washing the skin with soap and water helps to stop them spreading.

Keeping your skin clean with soap and water is important for your general health. Soap can dry your skin up by destroying the natural oils in it. If you have dry skin, apply moisturising cream or lotion after you wash.

Sunbathe with care – never stay in the sun for long and always apply a protective sun oil or cream.

ANTISEPTICS

Antiseptics are chemicals that are used to kill germs on the human body. They prevent wounds going septic (getting infected). Liquid antiseptics are usually used to clean wounds. When the wound is clean, antiseptic creams are put on before a bandage or a sticking plaster. They help to keep the wound free from germs.

At the slightest whiff of antiseptic Virulus takes flight. That's because he and his friends, the ghastly bacteria, will be killed if they come in touch with antiseptics. One type of antiseptic, hydrogen peroxide, was discovered by the French scientist Thenard in 1818.

Antiseptic

If it hurts...

antiseptic. That will get rid of dirt and kill germs. After that, dry the area with gauze. If it isn't bleeding too much, it's best not to cover the wound but to leave it exposed to the air. It will form a scab more quickly if it is left uncovered. If you have to cover it because it is bleeding a lot, apply a piece of gauze or some other medicated bandaging such as a sticking

Hints and tips

You've probably had your own share of small wounds, cuts or grazes. They happen easily. What should you do when these injuries happen?
First, wash the wound with lots of clean water and soap, or, better still, with an

Cuts and grazes happen easily if you lead an active life. However small the wound, it is always important to clean it properly. As you clean it, try not to drag dirt from the edge of the wound into the centre. Its best to clean around the edge first and work your way to the centre. Wash your hands before you begin, and use soap and water or antiseptic lotion to clean the wound.

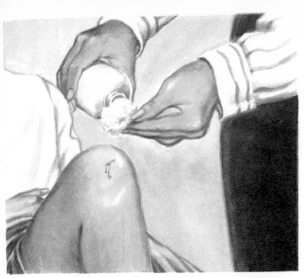

Dress the wound with the type of bandage that lets the air through. Air helps to dry the wound and germs do not like sun and fresh air. Take care to seal the dressing properly with sticking plaster to prevent dust getting into the wound. Your body will do the rest. A scab will form over the wound and new skin will begin to grow across it.

As soon as the wound has dried out and begins to form a scab, remove the sticking plaster so the natural healing process can take place.

A healthy, well-balanced diet keeps your body working efficiently. It helps your body's defence system to fight infection, and will also help your body to heal itself quickly.

plaster which doesn't stick to the wound. If the wound is large or deep, it should be seen by a doctor, because it may need stitching. The stitches hold the skin together and help it to heal. Try to see a doctor as quickly as you can – within six hours if possible. You should also see a doctor if the wound is very dirty or infected. Make sure you get regular tetanus injections. They prevent tetanus, a dangerous paralysing disease which may occur when an open wound has come into contact with dirt or rusty metal.

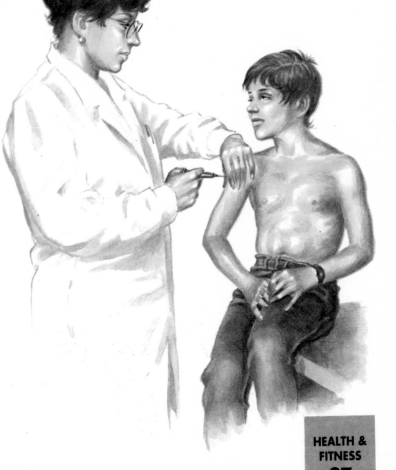

KEY WORDS

Acne – an eruption of spots mainly on the face and on the back of the shoulders. It is caused by blockage of the hair follicles and sebaceous glands

Antibiotics – drugs used to help fight infection

Antiseptics – chemicals used to kill germs on the body

Dermis – the second layer of skin, made of elastic fibres that give skin its stretchiness

Epidermis – the top layer of skin. It is waterproof and protects the body

Gauze – thin, sterilized (free of germs) bandaging material

Hypodermis – a fatty layer beneath the dermis and epidermis. It contains fat to protect and keep you warm

Keratin – a kind of protein found in skin, nails and hair

Melanin – the substance that protects skin from harmful rays of sun and gives skin its colour

Peroxide – the chemical substance containing water and oxygen, used as an antiseptic

Phagocytes – cells that help the body's defence mechanisms. They 'eat' germs and destroy them

Sebaceous glands – glands that produce oil to keep your skin and hair moist

Sensory receptors – nerve endings in the skin that detect pressure, pain and temperature and send messages to the brain

Sweat glands – glands that produce salty sweat to cool down the surface of the skin

Toxins – poisons given off by germs

Albert Barillé (pictured left) is the author of this fascinating series of books. The human body is a series of complex systems and mechanisms, so to make it easier for you to understand how the body works, Barillé created The Professor, Captain Courageous, Globus, Toxicus and Virulus, plus many other colourful cartoon characters, to show you around. The Professor and his friends guide you through the body, explaining how it works in a clear and simple way that makes it fun.

PARTS OF YOUR MODEL

This will help you to identify all the pieces that go together to make your model.

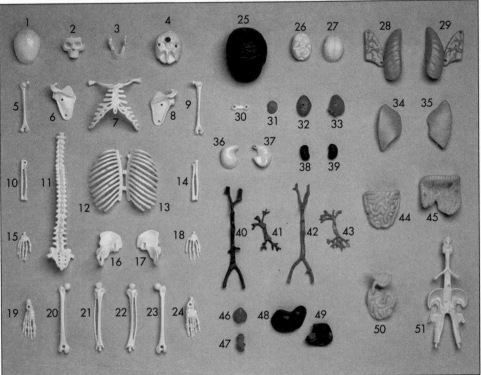

1 Cranium

2 Front of skull

3 Jawbone

4 Base of skull

5 Right humerus

6 Left shoulder blade

7 Sternum

8 Right shoulder blade

9 Left humerus

10 Right radius and ulna

11 Spinal column

12 Right rib cage

13 Left rib-cage

14 Left radius and ulna

15 Bones of right hand

16 Right pelvic bone

17 Left pelvic bone

18 Bones of left hand

19 Bones of right foot

20 Right femur

21 Right tibia and fibula

22 Left tibia and fibula

23 Left femur

24 Bones of left foot

25 Hair

26 Bottom part of brain

27 Top part of brain

28 Left lung

29 Right lung

30 Eyes

31 Spleen

32 Back of heart

33 Front of heart

34 Right pleura

35 Left pleura

36 Front of stomach

37 Back of stomach

38 Right kidney

39 Left kidney

40 Principal veins

41 Pulmonary veins

42 Principal arteries

43 Pulmonary arteries

44 Front of small intestine

45 Large intestine

46 Bladder

47 Anal passage

48 Front of liver

49 Back of liver

50 Pancreas and back of small intestine

51 Windpipe, gullet and cavities for the kidneys

Published by
Orbis Publishing
Griffin House
161 Hammersmith Road
London W6 8SD

UK & REPUBLIC OF IRELAND
Customer Services
If you have any queries on HOW MY BODY WORKS, please telephone 0990 - 673331.
Subscriptions
You can arrange to have your issues sent directly to your home at no extra cost. For details phone 0990 - 673331 (Mon-Fri, 9am-5pm). Credit card orders accepted.
Back Issues
These can be ordered from your newsagent. Alternatively, telephone 0990 - 673331 (Mon-Fri, 9am-5pm), or write to: Back Issues Department, HOW MY BODY WORKS, Orbis Publishing Ltd, PO Box 1, Hastings TN35 4TJ. Credit card orders accepted. When ordering please enclose:
1. Your name, address and postcode.
2. The issue number(s) and the number of copies of each issue you require.
3. Your payment of the cover price plus 50p per copy p&p. Make cheques/postal orders payable to Orbis Publishing Ltd.

AUSTRALIA
Back Issues (03) 9805 1700 Write to: Gordon and Gotch Ltd, PO Box 290, Burwood, VIC 3125. Please enclose cover price plus $1 per issue p&h.

NEW ZEALAND
Back Issues Telephone (09) 274 6700 for details or write to: Netlink Distribution Co, Private Bag 47906, Ponsonby, Auckland.

MALTA, SINGAPORE & MALAYSIA
Back Issues These can be ordered through your newsagent.

SOUTH AFRICA
Back Issues Telephone (011) 477 7391 for details, or write to: Back Issues Department, Republican News Agency, PO Box 16034, Doornfontein 2028. Please enclose cover price plus 2 Rand per issue p&h.
Subscriptions
Telephone: (011) 652 1888 for details, or write to: HOW MY BODY WORKS, Knowledge Ltd, Private Bag X13, Centurion 0046
© Procidis Albert Barillé
© 1996 Orbis Publishing Ltd, London

N2 96 10 10
ISBN 0 7489 3905 9

Printed in EC by Officine Grafiche De Agostini, Novara